STATUE
OF
LIBERTY

Keli Sipperley

Educational Media

rourkeeducationalmedia.com

Before Reading:

Building Academic Vocabulary and Background Knowledge

Before reading a book, it is important to tap into what your child or students already know about the topic. This will help them develop their vocabulary, increase their reading comprehension, and make connections across the curriculum.

1. *Look at the cover of the book. What will this book be about?*
2. *What do you already know about the topic?*
3. *Let's study the Table of Contents. What will you learn about in the book's chapters?*
4. *What would you like to learn about this topic? Do you think you might learn about it from this book? Why or why not?*
5. *Use a reading journal to write about your knowledge of this topic. Record what you already know about the topic and what you hope to learn about the topic.*
6. *Read the book.*
7. *In your reading journal, record what you learned about the topic and your response to the book.*
8. *After reading the book complete the activities below.*

Content Area Vocabulary
Read the list. What do these words mean?

alliance
authoritarian
beacon
centennial
commissioned
cooperative
counterparts
dedicated
enlightenment
immigrants
independence
representatives

After Reading:

Comprehension and Extension Activity

After reading the book, work on the following questions with your child or students in order to check their level of reading comprehension and content mastery.

1. *In what way was the Statue of Liberty a joint effort between the United States and France? (Summarize)*
2. *Who is the sonnet referring to when it states "give me your tired, your poor, your huddled masses?" (Infer)*
3. *What does the Statue of Liberty symbolize? (Summarize)*
4. *How would you describe the Statue of Liberty to someone who has never seen it? (Visualize)*
5. *What were some of the challenges in constructing the Statue of Liberty? (Asking questions)*

Extension Activity

Money was desperately needed by the American people in order to complete the pedestal for the statue. Write an opinion piece urging people to either donate or not to donate that will be sent to Joseph Pulitzer to publish in the *World*.

TABLE OF CONTENTS

A Gift of Friendship 4

The American Dream 6

Getting the United States Onboard 9

A Monumental Undertaking 18

How to Visit 26

Timeline 28

Glossary 30

Index 31

Show What You Know 31

Websites to Visit. 31

About the Author. 32

A GIFT OF FRIENDSHIP

Have you ever given a gift to a friend to show that you care about them?

A gift of friendship to the United States from the people of France became one of the most famous symbols in the world.

Standing tall and welcoming in the New York Harbor, the Statue of Liberty symbolizes French admiration for American freedom. It was meant to serve as a reminder of the friendship the two nations formed during America's fight for **independence**.

It was the people of the two nations, and not the governments, that made the statue possible. Citizens of both nations worked for 21 years to bring Lady Liberty to America.

Since she was unveiled in 1886, Lady Liberty has come to symbolize much more than the **alliance** between France and the United States. Facing east toward incoming ships with her torch raised lighting the way, the Statue of Liberty was often the first thing **immigrants** saw as they entered the harbor on their way to a new life in America.

This gift of friendship became a **beacon** of hope and a symbol of freedom to the world.

THE AMERICAN DREAM

On a summer evening in 1865, a group of friends gathered at the home of Édouard de Laboulaye for a dinner party in France. The intellectuals and artists at the party were happy that the United States of America had ended the Civil War and abolished slavery with the adoption of the Thirteenth Amendment.

The friends also admired America for its democratic government, which allowed citizens to vote for their **representatives**.

Freedom Fact!

The dinner party was held a few months after United States President Abraham Lincoln was assassinated, which saddened many French people. They felt the world had lost a living symbol of freedom.

At the time, France was under the oppressive rule of Napoleon III and in the middle of its own revolution. Those gathered at the party thought of America as a symbol of hope for freedom and democracy.

Laboulaye wanted to create a monument for the United States to celebrate its upcoming **centennial** anniversary. The centennial anniversary in 1876 would mark 100 years since the United States declared its independence from British rule.

Édouard de Laboulaye
(1811-1883)

The monument, Laboulaye hoped, would inspire the French people to demand a government free from oppressive **authoritarian** leadership. An authoritarian government favors strict obedience over personal freedom.

One guest, a young sculptor named Frédéric Auguste Bartholdi, was especially excited about the idea of a monument.

The dinner party ended, and decades of work began.

Frédéric Auguste Bartholdi (1834-1904)

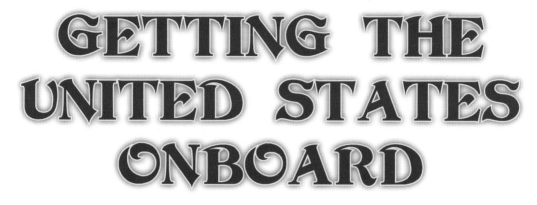

GETTING THE UNITED STATES ONBOARD

In 1870, Bartholdi began designing "Liberty Enlightening the World," the Statue of Liberty's official name.

"Go to see that country," Laboulaye told Bartholdi. "Propose to our friends over there to make with us a monument, a common work, in remembrance of the ancient friendship of France and the United States."

In 1871, the sculptor sailed to America to scout out a location for his colossal monument. As he entered New York Harbor, he saw Bedloe's Island. Bartholdi wanted the statue to rise out of the island's star-shaped Fort Wood, a military fort used during the Revolutionary War.

Freedom Fact!

Bartholdi considered New York the gateway to America because many immigrants entered through its harbor.

During his visits to America, Bartholdi shared the idea for the monument. He carried sketches of his design and a small model of the statue.

In order to build the monument, Bartholdi needed American citizens to work with the French people. The statue was designed to be a **cooperative** project. France would build the statue, and the United States would build her pedestal.

Bartholdi convinced some Americans to support the idea, including U.S. President Ulysses S. Grant.

France constructed the statue.

The United States constructed the pedestal that Lady Liberty stands on.

Ulysses S. Grant (1822-1885)

Laboulaye and his dinner party guests had hoped to raise Lady Liberty in time for America's centennial in 1876. Unfortunately, the effort took longer and cost more than expected. Still, those **dedicated** to the statue remained committed to bringing the monument to America.

In 1876, many Americans gathered to celebrate the one-hundredth anniversary of the signing of the Declaration of Independence in Philadelphia.

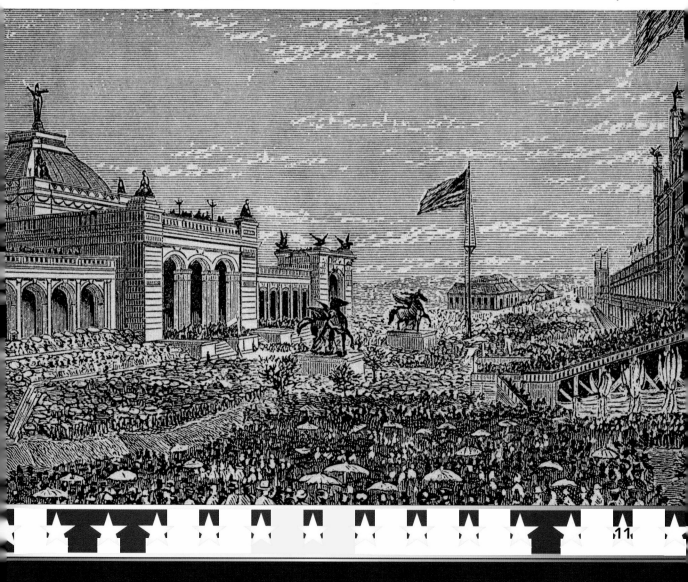

Bartholdi and his workmen were already building the 151 foot (46 meter) copper statue. But many Americans worried that such a giant statue would be impossible to finish. They hesitated to invest in the pedestal before there was proof that the French would be able to deliver the statue.

Lady Liberty was constructed at Bartholdi's workshop in Paris. At this point in her construction, Bartholdi had not yet added the rays to her crown.

In 1876, the French gave their American **counterparts** a hand.

The Statue of Liberty's right arm and torch were shipped to America. They were promptly put on display at the Centennial Exposition in Philadelphia and at Madison Square Park in New York City.

Lady Liberty's head and shoulders were exhibited in France the same year.

Exposition, 1876

The statue's head on exhibit at the Paris World's Fair, 1878

The displays did the trick! The American Committee for the Statue of Liberty formed in 1877. The committee worked to raise money for the statue's pedestal.

Events were held in both countries to raise money for the monument. All funds came from the citizens. No funding came from either government.

To raise funds, the American Committee of the Statue of Liberty sold miniature statuettes based on Bartholdi's model.

In France, plays and operas were held to raise money for the statue. Because it was allowed for artistic causes, French law allowed a lottery to be held to raise funds. The statue's total cost of $250,000 was raised by 1882, entirely by the French people.

In the United States, the funds trickled in. The American committee staged theatrical productions, art exhibits, auctions, and even boxing matches to raise money.

Bartholdi's Paris workshop

In 1882, architect Richard Hunt was **commissioned** by the committee to design the statue's pedestal. It took two years and plenty of rejections before his design was accepted. He donated his $1,000 paycheck back to the committee to help pay for the construction costs.

Workers constructed the pedestal from concrete and covered the outside with granite.

Work on the pedestal began in 1884 but the American committee soon ran out of money. Fundraising fizzled. There was not enough to pay for the pedestal's completion.

Then, Joseph Pulitzer, the owner and editor of the *World*, promised to publish the name of any person who gave money to the cause.

Joseph Pulitzer
(1847-1911)

Though most of the donations were less than a dollar each, the newspaper quickly raised more than $100,000.

The money allowed the committee to resume construction not a moment too soon: Lady Liberty was on her way.

A MONUMENTAL UNDERTAKING

Crossing rough seas, which nearly sank her to the ocean floor, the completed Statue of Liberty sailed across the Atlantic. The statue arrived at Bedloe's Island in 300 pieces on June 17, 1885.

The statue's arrival was met with great excitement. Unfortunately, the American people would have to wait more than a year to see the enormous monument in its full glory.

Newspapers reported the arrival of the statue on the French transport steamer, Isere.

On her voyage across the Atlantic Ocean, the boat carrying Lady Liberty nearly sank in a storm.

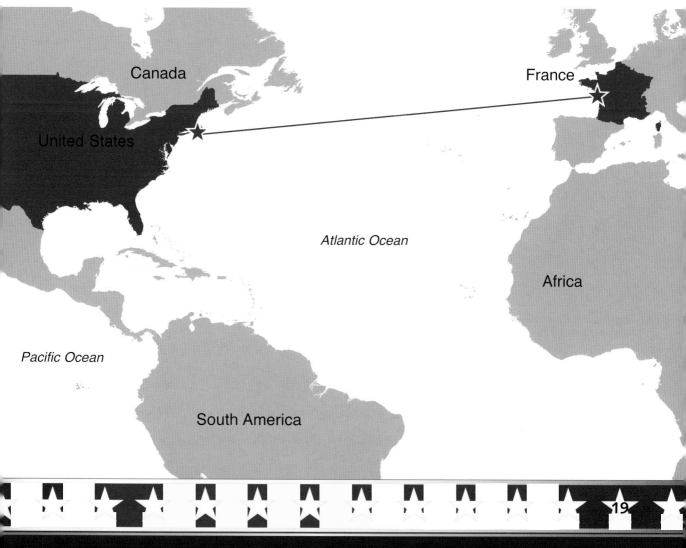

Packed in more than 200 crates, the copper pieces sat for nearly a year. They could not be touched until the pedestal was completed in April 1886. It then took four months for the copper and steel structure to be reassembled atop the pedestal.

YORK.—PREPARING THE STATUE OF "LIBERTY," ON BEDLOE'S ISLAND, FOR THE FORMAL UNVEILING ON OCTOBER 28TH.—PRESENT CONDITION OF
FROM A SKETCH BY A STAFF ARTIST.—SEE PAGE 535.

Freedom Fact!

Symbols Built into the Statue of Liberty

- *The torch symbolizes **enlightenment**, illuminating the path to freedom.*

- *The crown's seven spikes represent the seven seas and seven continents of the world.*

- *The tablet in the statue's left hand is a book of law inscribed in Roman numerals with the date of America's independence. The shape of the tablet is called a keystone, a stone that keeps the others together in construction. It symbolizes the importance of law in maintaining freedom and democracy.*

- *There are broken chains at the statue's feet that can only be seen from the air. They symbolize freedom from slavery and oppression.*

Ten years after the United States' centennial, "Liberty Enlightening the World" was unveiled. On October 28, 1886 a dedication ceremony was led by United States President Grover Cleveland and the monument's creator, Frédéric Bartholdi.

"We will not forget that Liberty has here made her home, nor shall her chosen altar be neglected," President Cleveland said.

President Grover Cleveland (1837-1908)

Freedom Fact!

Alexandre Gustave Eiffel, creator of the famous Eiffel Tower in Paris, designed the Statue of Liberty's spine. The sturdy steel framework inside the monument secures it against the elements, including hurricane-force winds. Four iron posts running from its base to the top support the weight of the statue.

American poet Emma Lazarus wrote a sonnet, *The New Colossus*, in 1883 for a statue fundraiser. It was engraved on a plaque and placed on the pedestal in 1903.

Emma Lazurus
(1849-1887)

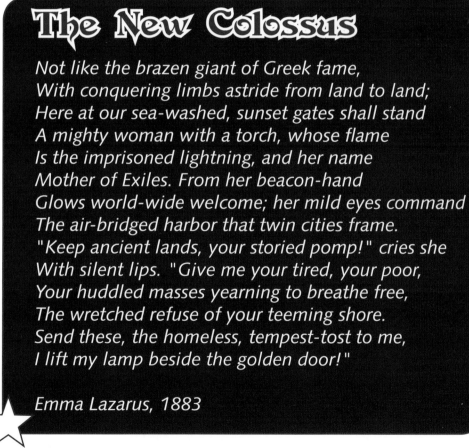

The New Colossus

Not like the brazen giant of Greek fame,
With conquering limbs astride from land to land;
Here at our sea-washed, sunset gates shall stand
A mighty woman with a torch, whose flame
Is the imprisoned lightning, and her name
Mother of Exiles. From her beacon-hand
Glows world-wide welcome; her mild eyes command
The air-bridged harbor that twin cities frame.
"Keep ancient lands, your storied pomp!" cries she
With silent lips. "Give me your tired, your poor,
Your huddled masses yearning to breathe free,
The wretched refuse of your teeming shore.
Send these, the homeless, tempest-tost to me,
I lift my lamp beside the golden door!"

Emma Lazarus, 1883

Thousands of people attended the celebration to welcome the 151 foot (46 meter) woman. She would soon welcome the millions of immigrants entering New York Harbor, making their way to the land of liberty.

The monument became a symbol of American compassion and the nation's willingness to take in the world's "tired, poor and huddled masses."

In 1886, Edward Moran memorialized the completion of Lady Liberty in his painting, Unveiling the Statue of Liberty.

Freedom Fact!

Facts about the Statue of Liberty

- *The monument was modeled after Libertas, the Roman Goddess of Liberty.*

- *The height from the base of the pedestal to the tip of the statue's torch is 305 feet, 6 inches (93 meters).*

- *Lady Liberty has a 35 foot (10.6 meter) waistline and would need a size 879 shoe!*

- *The 300 sheets of copper covering of the Statue of Liberty is less than the thickness of two pennies.*

- *In 50 mile-per-hour (80 kilometer-per-hour) winds, the statue sways 3 inches (7.6 centimeters) and the torch shifts 5 inches (12.7 centimeters).*

- *The Statue of Liberty is hit by about 600 bolts of lightning every year.*

HOW TO VISIT

Visitors to the statue must arrive by ferry. Ferries leave from Liberty State Park in New Jersey and Battery Park in New York City.

The entrance to the statue is through the walls of Fort Wood. Visitors may wish to go inside the statue. They can climb all the way to the statue's crown and get a bird's eye view of New York Harbor.

From the crown's 25 windows, visitors can get a 360-degree, panoramic view of Ellis Island, New York, New Jersey, and the New York Harbor. That means you can see all the way around the statue, from every direction!

Freedom Fact!

The torch has been closed to visitors since 1916, when an explosion on a nearby island damaged the torch arm and part of the crown.

Inside the statue lobby, you can see the original torch. The torch was replaced during a restoration project in the mid-1980s. The new torch features a copper flame covered in 24 karat gold.

About 4 million people from all over the world visit the Statue of Liberty each year. They go to get a close-up look at this lasting symbol of liberty and friendship.

Freedom Fact!

When the statue was constructed in 1886, its copper exterior was the color of an American penny. Over the next 30 years, the copper combined with oxygen in the air and formed a green coating that protects the copper from corrosion.

TIMELINE

1865 —— *The idea for a monument commemorating the friendship between France and the United States is proposed.*

1875 —— *The Franco-American Union is formed. The Union makes plans and secures funds for the statue. Édouard de Laboulaye is named president of the Union.*

1876 —— *The statue's hand and torch are completed and sent to the United States. They are displayed at the Centennial Exposition in Philadelphia.*

1878 —— *The statue's head and shoulders are completed. They are displayed for first time at the Paris Universal Exposition.*

1882 —— *Édouard de Laboulaye dies.*

1883 —— *Emma Lazarus writes* The New Colossus *for an art and literary auction to raise funds for the statue's pedestal.*

June 17
1885 ━━━ *The Statue of Liberty arrives on American soil.*

October 28
1886 ━━━ *The Statue of Liberty is unveiled by Frédéric Auguste Bartholdi and dedicated by President Grover Cleveland at a ceremony.*

1903 ━━━ *Emma Lazarus's sonnet* The New Colossus *is engraved on a plaque and placed on the inner wall of the pedestal of the Statue of Liberty.*

October 15
1924 ━━━ *President Calvin Coolidge declares the Statue of Liberty and the island a national monument.*

1933 ━━━ *The National Park Service assumes responsibility for care of the statue.*

1956 ━━━ *Bedloe's Island is renamed Liberty Island.*

1982 ━━━ *President Ronald Reagan establishes a commission to restore the statue for its 100th anniversary celebration in 1986.*

GLOSSARY

alliance (uh-LYE-uhns): a union between people, groups, or countries; a relationship in which people agree to work together

authoritarian (uh-THOR-i-tay-REE-uhn): a government in which the leaders and not the people have the final authority

beacon (BEE-kuhn): a light or warning signal used to guide ships

centennial (sen-TEN-ee-uhl): a one-hundredth anniversary

commissioned (kuh-MISH-und): appointed; assigned to a task or function

cooperative (koh-AH-pruh-tiv): working together

counterparts (KOUN-tur-pahrts): people whose jobs are the same as those from another organization

dedicated (DED-i-kated): committed to a project; having put a lot of time and work into something

enlightenment (en-LYE-tuhn-ment): giving someone knowledge or understanding

immigrants (IM-uh-gruhnts): people who come to a country

independence (in-DE-pen-dens): freedom from outside control or support

representatives (rep-ri-SEN-tuh-tivs): those who act on behalf of another through delegated authority

INDEX

American Committee for the Statue
of Liberty 14, 15, 17

Bartholdi, Frédéric Auguste 8, 9,
10, 12, 22

Bedloe's Island 9, 18

Civil War 6

Cleveland, Grover 22

Fort Wood 9, 26

Laboulaye, Édouard 6, 7, 8, 9, 11

Lazarus, Emma 23

Lincoln, Abraham 6

Napoleon III 7

Pulitzer, Joseph 17

slavery 6, 21

Thirteenth Amendment 6

U.S. independence 4, 7, 21

SHOW YOU KNOW

1. What does the Statue of Liberty symbolize?
2. How has its symbolic meaning changed over time?
3. What symbols are incorporated into the statue's design?
4. How did the people of France and America work together to build the statue?
5. Why was Bedloe's Island chosen for the statue's location?

WEBSITES TO VISIT

www.statueofliberty.org
www.nps.gov/stli/forkids/index.htm
www.thestatueofliberty.com/liberty_games.html

ABOUT THE AUTHOR

Keli Sipperley is a multimedia journalist and children's book author in Tampa, Florida. She enjoys writing stories about interesting moments, fun places, and people who help others in their communities. She has two sons and two daughters who love reading and writing as much as she does.

Meet The Author!
www.meetREMauthors.com

PHOTO CREDITS: page 4 © Richard Semik; page 5 © Alex Gulevich; page 7 © Truchelut, Rue de Grammont Paris; page 8 © Napoleon Sarony; page 10, 11, 13, 14, 15, 17, 18, 20, 22 © Library of Congress; page 12, 16 © Statue of Liberty National Park Service; page 22 © Gustave Eiffel; page 23 © American Jewish Historical Society; page 24 © Edward Moran

Edited by: Jill Sherman

Cover design by: Nicola Stratford, www.nicolastratford.com
Interior design by: Renee Brady

Library of Congress PCN Data

Statue of Liberty / Keli Sipperly
(Symbols of Freedom)
ISBN 978-1-62717-743-6 (hard cover)
ISBN 978-1-62717-865-5 (soft cover)
ISBN 978-1-62717-976-8 (e-Book)
Library of Congress Control Number: 2014935669

Printed in the United States of America, North Mankato, Minnesota

Also Available as: